The
Wild Outdoors

GO FRESHWATER FISHING!

by
Lisa M. Bolt Simons

CAPSTONE PRESS
a capstone imprint

Captivate is published by Capstone Press, an imprint of Capstone.
1710 Roe Crest Drive, North Mankato, Minnesota 56003
www.capstonepub.com

Library of Congress Cataloging-in-Publication Data
Names: Simons, Lisa M. B., 1969- author.
Title: Go freshwater fishing! / by Lisa M. Bolt Simons.
Description: North Mankato, Minnesota : Capstone Press, [2022] |
Series: The wild outdoors | Includes bibliographical references and
index. | Audience: Ages 8-11 | Audience: Grades 4-6 | Summary:
"Freshwater fishing is the perfect combination of relaxation and
excitement. When you're not peacefully looking out at the water,
you're reeling in the big one! Readers will learn all about the gear
and skills they need to help them reel in the fish they're hoping to
hook!"— Provided by publisher.
Identifiers: LCCN 2021004228 (print) | LCCN 2021004229 (ebook) |
ISBN 9781663906076 (hardcover) | ISBN 9781663920515 (paperback) |
ISBN 9781663906045 (pdf) | ISBN 9781663906069 (kindle edition)
Subjects: LCSH: Fishing—Juvenile literature. | Freshwater fishes—
Juvenile literature.
Classification: LCC SH445 .S525 2022 (print) | LCC SH445 (ebook) |
DDC 799.1/1—dc23
LC record available at https://lccn.loc.gov/2021004228
LC ebook record available at https://lccn.loc.gov/2021004229

Image Credits
Alamy: Craig Larcom, 13, SnapTPhotography, 25; Getty Images: Larry
Williams & Associates, 8; Newscom: Don Mason Blend Images, 29;
Shutterstock: Ad Oculos, 16, Dan Thornberg, 23, Iakov Filimonov, 24, CLP
Media, 28, goodluz, 17, 19, GROGL, 27, Marzolino, 7, Monkey Business
Images, 9, Nutdanai Vipassakulsuk, 15, Photos BrianScantlebury, 5,
Rocksweeper, Cover, 1, sirtravelalot, 20, vitec, 12, Volodymyr Maksymchuk,
11, Zheltyshev, 14

Editorial Credits
Editor: Mandy Robbins; Designer: Jennifer Bergstrom; Media Researcher:
Jo Miller; Production Specialist: Tori Abraham

Table of Contents

Words in **bold** are in the glossary.

FRESHWATER FISHING FUN

You're standing on a dock on a quiet morning. The sun is shining overhead. The sky is clear and blue. The water gently rocks the dock. You're wearing shorts, a t-shirt, sunglasses, and a hat. Your life jacket is nice and snug, and you smell of sunscreen.

You're getting ready to freshwater fish. You have a rod and reel. When you're ready, you **bait** the hook. You put the rod back over your shoulder and cast! The bait *plinks* into the water.

Now it's time to wait for the fish. How long will it be before a fish bites the bait? There! Your rod is bending! The fish is on your line! Time to reel in your catch!

Be sure to wear a life jacket when fishing from a dock.

Chapter 1

FISHING FIRSTS

Many people once had to fish to survive. Stories about fishing have been found in art and writings around the world.

One of the first fishing tools was the hook. The first hooks were made out of stone, bone, or wood. Then copper and bronze were used for hooks. They were probably attached to tree branches or sticks. The fishing line was made from material found in animals or plants.

Fishing **tackle** improved over time. In the 1600s a loop or ring was added to the end of the pole. The line could run through this loop or ring. It helped with casting and catching a fish. Because there was more line, the reel was invented. It stored the extra line.

An 1864 print of Chontaquiros people fishing in present-day Peru

FACT

Ancient carvings in Cosquer Cave in southern France show people using spears called harpoons to kill sea animals. These carvings were made more than 1,600 years ago.

Today, fishing, or angling, is a popular sport. Almost anywhere there is water, there are fish. From the smallest streams to the biggest lakes, you can go freshwater fishing. You can fish from the shores of a pond, lake, or river, or from a boat or a dock.

Fishing is a sport for all ages. You can also fish with friends and family all year long! No matter who you go with, always be sure to have a trusted adult with you.

You'll need to decide which equipment, or tackle, to use. Your rod, reel, line, bait, and **lures** will vary. It depends on which **species** of fish you want to catch. Being in nature and challenging yourself to try to catch a fish is what makes angling enjoyable!

FACT

Nearly 40 million Americans spend one day a year fishing! These anglers spend about $45 billion on fishing-related expenses every year!

Chapter 2

TACKLE TIME

Do you want to fish with a rod or a pole? That's your first decision when it comes to tackle. Fishing poles are made out of natural material like wood. Fishing rods are modern. They are made out of material like **fiberglass**.

There are different types of poles and rods. Spinning rods are popular. They have reels under the rod. They are used to mainly catch sport fish like trout. Bait casting and closed-spin casting rods have reels above the handle. More advanced anglers use these rods. **Carbon fiber** rods are often used by professionals. Telescopic rods adjust to be long or short. A rod as long as 20 feet (6 meters) can shorten to just 18 inches (45 centimeters) to travel more easily. Ultra-light rods are for smaller fish such as bass. They are short and use light lures and flies.

spinning rods

Bait fishing or lure fishing is your next decision. Bait is what's found in nature—worms, **minnows**, and insects. Lures are man-made fishing bait. Some lures are painted to look like they're from nature.

Bait such as worms catch most freshwater fish. Even professional anglers use worms. Minnows are another popular bait. They are the best bait for fish that stay near the shore. Pike, bass, catfish, and walleyes eat minnows. Crappies, pronounced "croppies," also dine on minnows.

Earthworms are a popular fishing bait.

Leeches in a bait container

More surprising bait include ladybugs, crickets, dragonflies, and more insects. Sunfish and trout like this bait. Bass have been caught with crawfish, frogs, and crabs. Crappies also enjoy **crustaceans**. Smallmouth bass like leeches.

Finding Freshwater Fish

Most of Earth is covered in water. But it's mostly salty ocean water. Less than 3 percent of Earth's water is fresh water. But almost half of the fish species lives in fresh water. There are more than 10,000 species of freshwater fish!

spinning lures

There are countless lures for fish. Different lures attract different species of fish.

Spinners are made of wire with a metal blade at the end. The spinning catches the eye of all kinds of fish.

Jigs have round metal heads. They can be plain or have feathers, plastic, or other materials. The different colors, weights, and shapes attract fish such as walleyes and perch.

Crank baits and swimbaits look like small fish. Bass and other fish who eat smaller fish are drawn to these lures.

Jerk-baits are also used with bass, pike, and musky. When the pole is jerked up, the lure moves quickly. It scares the fish, and the fish attacks it.

Poppers make water splash as the angler "pops" the lure back after the cast. These lures catch northern pike and walleye.

popper lure

Of course, your tackle isn't complete without fishing line. Fishing line is usually made of **nylon**. It comes in different pound test weights. The pound test describes how strong a line is. Fish can see heavy line in the water. But light line can break easily. You have to find a balance. Different rods, reels, baits, and lures work better with different types of lines. As with lures and bait, you must choose the line based on what fish you want to catch.

Fishing line comes in many colors.

Use a net to help scoop up the fish once you've reeled it in.

Never throw broken or used fishing line in the water. Line that is left behind can hurt or kill wildlife.

Optional equipment includes leaders, sinkers, and bobbers. This equipment could help your game plan to catch more fish. You might also take a net to bring the fish in!

Chapter 3

FISHING BASICS

Once you've got your tackle, you may need to buy a fishing license. Check with the state, province, or country where you live to see what is required. The money used to buy a license goes toward helping with **conservation** programs.

Once you have a license, there are five main ways to fish. Bait and lure fishing is probably the most well-known. Bait casting and spin casting use different kinds of reels, line, and bait. Fly fishing is when the angler uses a rod and a heavy line with a lure called a fly on the end. The angler snaps the fly at the end of the line on and off the water. Trolling is when the bait or the lure is in the water. It is pulled behind a boat very slowly.

Fly fishers often stand in the water as they fish.

FACT

Fly fishing dates back about 2,200 years. It began in Central Europe in modern-day Macedonia.

Fishing is a fun sport for all ages.

You've caught a fish! Now what?

Make sure the fish looks healthy. It should have clear eyes and red gills. Sick fish have sunken eyes and white or slimy gills. Eating an unhealthy fish can make you sick.

If you plan to eat your fish, you don't want the meat to spoil. You can have an adult clean it right away or use a stringer. A stringer is a rope that goes through the mouth and gills of live fish. Fish stay alive longer on a stringer. The stringer of fish stays in the water. Or you can use a live well or cooler filled with water.

Other anglers choose to catch and release. They catch a fish but then let it go. Catch and release can help a fish **ecosystem**.

Freshwater Fish Conservation

Fish conservation programs are important for freshwater fishing to be enjoyed for years to come. The U.S Fish & Wildlife Service's National Fish Passage Program helps fish reconnect with their natural habitats when rivers are reopened or obstacles are moved. The National Oceanic and Atmospheric Administration Fisheries help protect fish species. The World Wildlife Fund is helping to protect water ecosystems around the world.

Chapter 4

SAFETY FOR "REEL"

Having a fun fishing trip also means staying safe. Make sure you fish with a trusted adult. Always wear a life jacket on a dock or in a watercraft. You should also protect yourself from the sun and insects. It's often cool if you fish early in the morning. Dress in layers in case the temperature changes.

There are also other factors to consider. Know what the weather will be like. It can change quickly. Stay off private property and always protect wildlife.

Bring items for both comfort and emergency. You'll need water and snacks, especially for long days on the water. Maps and a cell phone are important to find your way. If you're fishing at night, bring a flashlight.

A boy uses a stringer to hold up his catch.

Anglers must be careful when handling hooks.

Fishing involves a lot of sharp objects. You need to be careful while having fun.

Hooks aren't just sharp at the end. They also have barbs, which are sharp points sticking out from the hook. Make sure you know where other anglers are when you cast. You don't want to hook them, too.

A fish can have sharp fins and scales. Have an adult help you when you are taking a fish off a hook.

Knives are used to clean fish, but let adults handle them. When fishing, knife blades should be covered and kept in a safe place.

If you fish while standing in water, be careful of stepping on sharp rocks or in deep holes. Also watch for swift-moving water.

The closer you stand to the shore, the safer you are from fast-moving currents.

Chapter 5

HITTING THE ICE

But what if it's winter and the water is frozen? You can go ice fishing!

Just as with other fishing, safety comes first. An adult needs to make sure the ice is thick enough. To walk on ice, it should be at least 4 inches (10 cm) thick. To drive a car or truck on ice, it should be at least 8 to 12 inches (20 to 30.5 cm) thick.

Make sure you wear warm clothes for ice fishing. You should also wear a life jacket. Some people also wear a whistle. They blow it if the ice starts to crack. Then someone can come help them get to safety.

Once you choose your spot on the ice, an adult will drill a hole that is 8 to 10 inches (20 to 25 cm) wide. Jigging with a bobber is the most common way to ice fish. Just put your bait or lure on your line and drop it in the hole!

Anglers use a tool called an auger to drill holes in the ice for ice fishing.

┌─ *FACT* ─

One of the most famous ice fishing contests in the world is held in Brainerd, Minnesota. Tens of thousands of anglers have competed there every January since 1991.

An angler holds a bluegill fish.

Let's Go Fishing!

No matter where or when you go, some of the best fishing is for panfish. Panfish include bluegills, crappies, perch, and sunfish. They're found in most lakes and streams. They're not picky about their bait.

Another popular fish is bass. There are largemouth and smallmouth bass. They're known for being fighters on the hook.

Other species include catfish, carp, striped bass, walleye, and trout. These fish are good for beginners and prized by professionals.

Fishing is a timeless sport with a lot of choices. Which rod? Which reel? Do you use bait or a lure? Most importantly, which fish do you want to catch? No matter your decisions, stay safe and have fun on the water freshwater fishing!

An angler holds a rainbow trout.

GLOSSARY

bait (BAYT)—a small amount of food put on a hook to attract a fish; also the action of putting the food on a fishing hook

carbon fiber (KAHR-buhn FY-buhr)—a strong, lightweight material made of very thin threads of carbon

conservation (kon-sur-VAY-shuhn)—the protection of animals and plants, as well as the wise use of what we get from nature

crustacean (cruh-STAY-shuhn)—a sea animal with an outer skeleton, such as a crab, lobster, or shrimp

ecosystem (EE-koh-sis-tuhm)—a group of animals and plants that work together with their surroundings

fiberglass (FY-buhr-glas)—a strong, lightweight material made from thin threads of glass

lure (LOOR)—a fake bait used in fishing

minnow (MIH-no)—a tiny freshwater fish

nylon (NYE-lon)—an artificial fiber that makes a very strong cloth

species (SPEE-sheez)—a group of plants or animals that share common characteristics

tackle (TAK-uhl)—the equipment that you need for a particular activity, such as fishing

READ MORE

Carpenter, Tom. *Freshwater Fishing.* Mendota Heights, MN.: North Star Editions, 2017.

Palmer, Andrea. *We're Going Freshwater Fishing.* New York: Rosen Publishing, 2017.

Willis, John. *Freshwater Fishing.* New York: Av2, 2020.

INTERNET SITES

Education and Kids: Fishes of Boneyard Creek
fishesofboneyardcreek.weebly.com/education-and-kids.html

Junior Ranger Let's Go Fishing!
nps.gov/subjects/fishing/junior-ranger-fishing.htm

Species for Beginner Anglers
in-fisherman.com/editorial/get-on-board-species-for-beginner-anglers/383327#replay

INDEX